Fifty Two

Celebrating 90 years of Brightlingsea Lido

Brightlingsea Lido

CASTLE PRIORY PRESS

First published in Great Britain in 2023 by Castle Priory Press, Brightlingsea

ISBN 978-1-915970-02-2

Copyright © Castle Priory Press, 2023
Cover design: Jane Langan
Cover illustration: c/o Brightlingsea History Hub archives

For all Lido users, everywhere

Contents

Introduction

This is my second year as Writer in Residence and I'm delighted to be joined by Becky Jackson and Chrissie Richards as Artists in Residence. Together, we have some exciting projects planned.

Since the release of the last anthology, the first of my series of books set in a fictional version of Brightlingsea ('Folly') has been released, having a successful launch as part of the first Brightlingsea Literary Festival. The second book is well underway and a third is in the planning stages.

We have also started the ball rolling with beginning to turn the Lido Cafe into a Creative Hub for the Community, when it's not in use as a cafe! We have run art and literature workshops, both for our Lido projects and also for the Brightlingsea Literary Festival (with WinterFest) and have more planned for the future.

This anthology is the result of our 90 Words Project, which ran throughout 2022 to celebrate the Lido's 90th birthday. We put out a call for people to contribute pieces of either 90 words or 90 characters about the Lido and each week, one was published on our Facebook page. Most were focused on the Lido, some referenced it as a part of the Brightlingsea landscape and some showed why sometimes the Lido can be a better option than the open sea!

There were so many lovely comments about them that we decided to turn them into a print book this year and Becky has provided illustrations to sit alongside them. We have also included a bonus poem and short story which came in too late for last year's anthology, but were both so good we asked permission to include them in this one! As with last year's anthology, none of this would have been possible without the contributions of some incredibly talented writers.

I continue to enjoy my one day a week working in the Lido café and I am immeasurably grateful to the staff for keeping me supplied with endless cups of coffee. I am also delighted that people continue to come down and talk to me about my writing, buy my books and ask for advice about their own writing or publishing questions. (I would also like to thank all the dog-owners who put up with me fussing over their dogs!)

If you'd like to talk to me about the anthology or any other writing-related matters, I can be found in a corner of the Lido Café most Fridays or you can contact me directly via email: **lidowriter@gmail.com**

As usual, I've written far too much, but rather than edit all my words away, I will leave you with this final thought. Whilst this anthology was created to celebrate 90 years of our Lido, the creative team behind it are very much looking to the future. We have plans for more literary and art workshops, so if you have something 'arty' or 'writery' that you'd love to learn more about, drop us a line and we'll see what we can come up with!

All that's left for me to say now is, 'Take the plunge, turn the page and enjoy!'

Ruth Loten

HISTORY

Lido: public open-air swimming pool or pleasure beach
(Concise Oxford Dictionary)

The golden age of British lidos was in the 1930s. As outdoor swimming grew in popularity, they sprang up all over the country, only to close again as it gradually fell out of fashion. In the early 21st century, there was a move to re-open many of them, as once again, people began to consider the physical and mental health benefits of swimming outside.

Brightlingsea Lido (originally Brightlingsea Open Air Swimming Bath) was built as part of a scheme designed to improve the recreational facilities in the town. It was funded by a grant from the government's Unemployment Grant Committee as part of a national effort to provide much needed work for unemployed men and the grand opening took place on 23rd June 1932.

However, by 2017 its future was very much in doubt as Tendring Council made the decision to close it. A group of volunteers came together with a very different plan in mind and the Lido was relaunched as a local enterprise in 2018. Funding was secured to improve the facilities and in spite of the best efforts of Covid-19, four years later, it's still going strong with plans for further improvements already set in motion.

Further details on the history and future plans for the Lido can be found in the information leaflet available in the Lido Café or on our website: **www.brightlingsealido.org**.

BRIGHTLINGSEA LIDO AT DUSK

By Hugh Morrison

From out the sepia past I thought I heard
The sound of children playing, as a bird
Hovered over dappled, sunlit cool
Blue waters of the municipal pool.

Was it the ghostly sound of childhoods gone?
No, just the cackling of the bird, upon
The nearby sea, on rippling, greyish-green
Waves which bore him, till no longer seen.

Born in an age of British civic pride
The Lido - for a people long denied
The simple joy of water and of sun
A pleasure, not for some, but everyone.

On buses, trams and cycles they would go
To Brixton, Brockwell Park, or Plymouth Hoe;
Clifton, Tooting Bec or Saltdean, happily
Ruislip, London Fields - or Brightlingsea.

Here the busy world's vain show is hushed;

Here no money-changers throng, no rushed
And frantic roar of city crowds is heard
Only the weightless laughter of a bird.

Across the years, the Lido has remained
Though tyrants rose and fell, and Empires waned;
Wars raged, and men saw fortunes lost and won;
Its waters stand, still, gleaming in the sun.

90 Words or 90 Characters

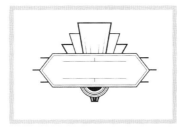

THE LIDO: 90 YEARS

R.E. LOTEN

Ninety years of watching
people swimming up and down
And still the Lido thrives. Hooray!!

3rd January

LIDO EARLY MORNING PROTOCOL

SUE SHEPPARD

Book.
QR code to hand.
No looking at 'temperature of the day' signage.
Ignore volunteer's 'I admire your bravery' comments.
Prepare 'exit care package' before entering water (supersized towelling robe, hot drink and springy 'slip on' footwear for fast transit to hot showers).
Slowly acclimatise as you immerse – wet face helps.
Graceful entrance (or not), vocal effects permitted.
Swim, fast and furious, as it really 'only takes minutes to adjust'.
Utilise inevitable adrenalin surge.
Relax, reflect and enjoy the awakening of every sense.
Celebrate your resilience.
The day has begun.

10th January

WHO AM I?

Karen Hine

Who am I?
I like to prowl around the promenade day and night
I love to rest and sleep in cars and huts
I spend time slinking around the playground
In the mornings I go for breakfast at Batemans
At lunch I try my luck at the Lido
When the fair comes to town
I enjoy checking out all the rides
My friends and family like to keep an eye out for me
To make sure I don't get cat napped
Who am I?
I am Max the Brightlingsea Cat

17ᵗʰ January

TALES FROM THE LIDO

Shaun Phillips

A child ventures into the pool, he is happy now, the thrashing about of water to and fro with his best friend. A large tidal wave causing mayhem has just begun. The clear water becomes bubbles. It's so thick it becomes white round the edges. Who will thrash the hardest? The fastest? Who will have the last thrash? I am not stopping yet; let's look at mum. Lying on the striped sun bed, she is not calling us out yet. Yay! I see it through his eyes as his mother.

24ᵗʰ January

ROB @ LIDO NINETEEN NINETY SOMETHING

PAULINE SMITH

Summer, sponsored swim.
Dive in. Cold. So very cold
The face says it all

*31*st *January*

31st January

WINTER WAVES

HELENA NWAOKOLO

Twice daily
winter waves claim their place
perpetually
regaining the space they own
invading what others think is theirs
but is only borrowed

noisy gulls wait to squabble for titbits
winter waders, to dip for dinner
the snow white egret, to dine alone
among the mud and stones
where the shelled and squidgy creatures find their space

dogs and hardy swimmers wait
for their splashes
until the waves withdraw
and the winter birds return
while the lido water
still in its own space
shelters passing fowl
from stormy winter waves.

7th February

7th February

MURDER MYSTERY NIGHT

R.E. LOTEN

A body floats in the Lido.
Motionless limbs splayed.
The spotlight pivots.
Murder mystery night has begun!

14ᵗʰ February

COMMUNITY AROUND

D.H.L Hewa

Rubbing arms, gingerly stepping forward, letting water swirl up ankles, shins, calves, until it reaches chest. Gasping, heart drumming, fluttering. C..o..ld. Co..l..d. Col...d. F..o..c.us. Focus. Shimmering ripples reflecting sky, diving duck companions, swimming alongside. Deep, slow breaths, glide one length, two. Numb hands and feet, time to clamber out. Sun warming skin, steam rising from body, wet feet tread briskly on icy deck, towards a cold shower. Layering clothes back on, to a tingling body, sip hot water slowly, from flask cup. Warm, sharing stories with the swimming community around.

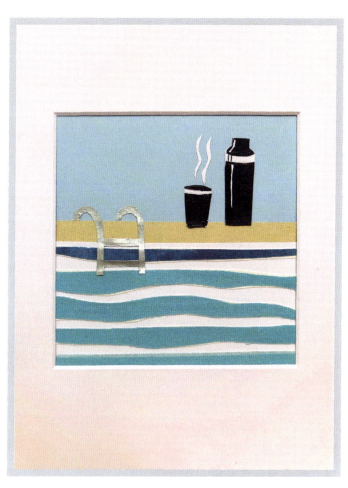

21ˢᵗ February

AWARDS NIGHT

R. E. LOTEN

We dressed up for awards night
Breath held. Fingers crossed.
Pipped at the post
But so very proud of our team.

28th February

WRITING WORKSHOP SUCCESS

R. E. Loten

Fingers tap laptop keys,
Pens dance across paper.
Ideas fly around the café.
Inspiration strikes. Hoorah!

7th March

MEMORIES OF
MY MUM
JACQUELINE BUCHANAN

My mum (Shirley Buchanan) was a PE teacher at the Colne High school in the 60's . She taught swimming at the pool alongside Rod James and Pete Currell. They believed that the pool was not a sanitary environment for people especially children to be swimming in. They started a campaign to 'clean the pool' and I remember her collecting water samples for analysis to prove their point and attending meetings with the local councillors at that time. I believe they were instrumental in the closure of the old pool.

14ᵗʰ March

WE LOVE THE LIDO

THE STEPHENS FAMILY

Wet!
Exceptionally cold!!

Looking forward to a friendly welcome; even lovelier if Max
the cat is there too.
Outdoor swimming feels healthy and fun whilst
Vigorous activity helps keep us warm, because it is
Exceedingly cold!!!

The Lido Llama and riding on their back.
Hot drinks to warm up,
Except in summer when ice-cream is better!

Laying back, floating beneath the endless sky.
Imagining the water to be tropical,
Despite swimming in the rain, then dashing home, soaked to
the bone.
Our Lido. One of our favourite places to be.

21ˢᵗ March

BRIGHTLINGSEA LIDO

ANNE BEERE

Breathtakingly blue, a real beauty at 90,
Reflecting the sun, white clouds and sky,
Inviting visitors from near and far.
Grab your towels and costumes,
Head on down, next to the Prom,
To the town's pride and joy,
Local landmark, at last back to life,
It's a shining azure gem,
Nothing else to compare in Essex,
Giving children and grown-ups
Such happy healthy fun,
Everyone can join in,
At Brightlingsea's awesome
Lovely and refreshing Lido!
Inflatables bring extra delight -
Dip, float, splash, swim or relax,
Oh, wonderful, precious pool!

28th March

BECOME A VOLUNTEER
Karen Hine

Make friends

Make a difference

Make a contribution

Make happiness

Make community

Make Brightlingsea Lido

4th April

THE POOL

Linda Moir

The pool saw my first spluttering swimming
Over wooden cracks where seaweed grows
In salty water my pride brimming and
Tiny crabs tickled toes

The pool saw Joan Collins draped on the slide
Glamour personified, oh teenage years
Transistor radios, whispers aside
Bikinis, sunbathing, lovelorn tears

The pool saw our sixth generation
Swimming, splashing, laughing together
Great grandchildren following family tradition
Precious memories lasting forever

The pool sees me now unsteady and grey
Taking the hands of my dear Daughters
Slowly they lead the way
Into familiar clear blue waters

11ᵗʰ April

OH HOW I LOVE THE LIDO

Peyton Filmer

The big day finally came,
I had set out with an aim,
I couldn't wait,
I didn't want to be late,
Oh, how I love the lido,

Wanting to learn how to float,
I looked like a big boat,
So many things to see,
It was all so new to me,
Oh, how I love the lido,

All my friends in sight,
I jumped in with all my might,
Swimming end to end,
Who knew what I could intend,
Oh, how I love the lido,

I really love the lido.

18ᵗʰ April

QUIZ NIGHT

R.E. LOTEN

Heads scratched, answers scribbled
Hastily confer
Was it...? That's right.
Another answer correct,
We won!

25th April

SWIMMING AT SPLASH POINT

STEPHANIE GREEN

The 'Beware Jellyfish' sign is ominous. There are oohh aahhh moments as I go carefully down the steps into the cool, cloudy water. Acclimatisation is gradual. The scent of the sea and the taste of brine on the lips makes it much more relaxing than swimming in chlorine-tinged water. Swim, float, head out towards the orange buoys away from the splashing of exuberant children. The sun above, the lapping of wavelets, the mewing of gulls. Then a squishy slap against my legs. I get out quicker than I got in.

*2ⁿᵈ **May***

COLD

Liz McManus

Cold
> So wet
> My toes freeze as I step in
> Knees bend to release
> My body to the cold

Breathe
> Open your skin
> Allow the water in
> Shiver and accept
> the wet

Arms sweep out
> To keep afloat
> Legs kick out
> To propel
> Me from the edge

.   .   .

A breath
    I bob
      Treading water to float
      I look up to see
      The water's edge

Surrounded by tiles
    All blue as the great sea
      Ripples of water distort
      The legs that
      I see

And then
    I realise
      That the water
      Is warm

*9ᵗʰ **May***

INSTRUCTIONS TO REMEMBER

LILY LAWSON

Cup my hand,
move it through the water,
make a circle with my arm back to the start,
do the same with the other arm,
one goes down and back,
one goes up and forward,
kick my legs alternately,
turn my head away from the arm entering the water,
breathe,
putting my face in the water is safe,
focus on what I'm doing,
never mind who's there,
block the noise out,
listen to my aunty's voice in my head,
I've got this,
I won't drown,
It's ok,
I can swim.

16th May

JET SKIS

Stephen Foster-Pilkington

Is it a Flymo spun out of control?
Or a hedge strimmer ripping an endless mow?
NO. it's a JET SKI DESIGNED TO DESTROY ALL
TRANQUILITY.
Is it safe? Well, that depends
If controlled by a bell complete with an end.
Its need for speed encounters no bounds
As it keeps chasing round and round and round.
Yet can it ever capture its tail?
While it guzzles between the sails?
But will thrill become kill
With the quest to be winner?
If it carelessly collides straight into a swimmer

23ʳᵈ May

GETTING THE LIDO READY

R.E. Loten

To get the Lido ready
Is really a team affair
With lots of jobs which must be done
Before the doors can open

We're all working very hard
To get the Lido ready
The smell of paint hangs in the air
The pool is almost done

In the café, rushing round
Tracy's team are working hard
To get the Lido ready
For the usual post-swim snack

The trustees do an amazing job
So do the volunteers
It's finally here. The doors swing open. We managed
To get the Lido ready.

30th May

THE BEATING HEART

BECK COLLETT

Step, slide, or splash into the water, gasping at the thrilling chill as it envelopes you in a hug. The beating heart of Brightlingsea Lido beats for all who care to hear it. 'Welcome back', it seems to say, or, 'good to meet you, friend.' Whether the weather is sunny or stormy, we'll be here. Rain? So what? You're going to get wet, aren't you? All part of the fun. Shrug off your clothes and cares, forget about everything for half an hour, or, half a day, and just *be*.

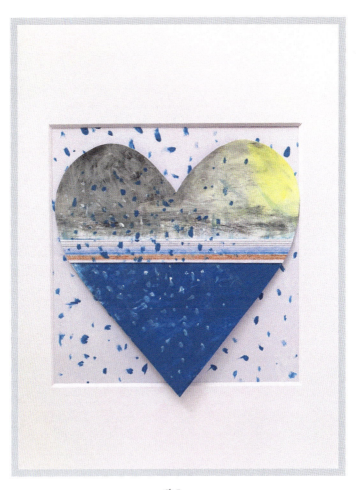

6th June

TALK OF THE TOWN

R.E. LOTEN

Not the usual sounds of laughter and splashing.
Instead, music pumps.
Echoes.
Listen! It's Talk Of The Town

13ᵗʰ June

ANNIVERSARY

R.E. Loten

90

90 characters.
90 words.
All leading to this.

Today marks 90 years
Of swimming,
Of community,
Of the Lido.

20th June

SOMETHING DIFFERENT

R.E. LOTEN

You can mark the solstice with a swim
Or try a new sport with Go-Tri
The Lido. Bringing the community together

*27ᵗʰ **June***

POSTCARD FROM BRIGHTLINGSEA

Linda Taglialavore

Iris,

Staying in Brightlingsea for a few days, good to get out of Croydon! The sun has shown its face once or twice which is nice. Staying at the Royal. Chicken and potatoes, ice cream, that sort of thing. Travelled down by train - left my hatbox in the rack which I am jolly furious about. Am writing this from poolside of the LIDO – the water looks most inviting. Have thought about chucking myself in, as quite frankly Derek is being an absolute beast.

Yours
Irene

4th July

CARNIVAL

KAREN HINE

The float is ready
With waves and volunteers
To wave to the crowd.
Brightlingsea waits.
It's carnival time!

11ᵗʰ July

FIREWORK SWIM

R.E. Loten

Colours fill the sky,
Sparkling on the water,
Beauty inverted.
Light reflected.
A different perspective.

18th July

ANTHOLOGY

R.E. Loten

The community came together
Creatives all united
To sing the praises of our lovely Lido
Anthology. Out now!

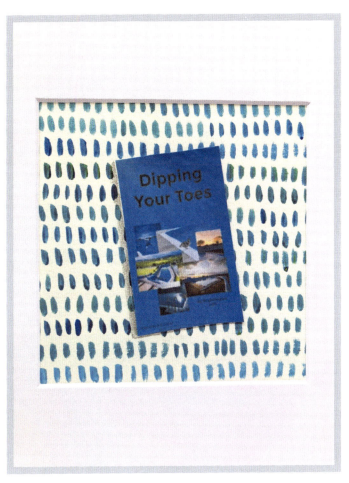

25th July

FIRST IN

CHRISTOPHER JAMES

I have the Lido to myself,
like a bird that owns the sky.
There's a sea beyond the wall
and a world beyond the sea.
But here, there's only me
on this blue tile that's fallen
to earth. I swim through the clouds.
Two others join me, not yet
enough to make a flock
or even a shoal, but enough
To start a summer. Soon,
others will come – families,
children, until I am only one
of many, swimming through the
heavens. Who knows the
lengths to which we will go.

*1ˢᵗ **August***

A LIDO CAFÉ DILEMMA

Stephen Foster-Pilkington

Does everyone back where you're from pronounce it scone?
Or might you find you're not alone in saying scone?
But some insist, on, on and on, it's scone and scone and scone
and scone.
Yet some come from homes that ask for scones
With tongs they select the one, their scone.
How their eyes roam to own their scone.
And while there's nothing wrong in scone?
Don't pick a bone if you hear scone.
But when they're gone, there's none – no scones
Don't moan or groan. Can't clone your scones.

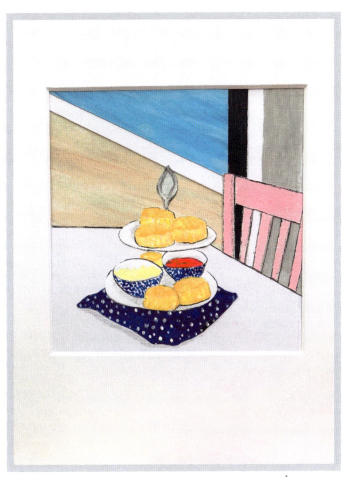

8th August

90 JUMPS: THE BIG SPLASH

R.E. LOTEN

90 people
all shapes and sizes.
Old and young
united by a common purpose.
A shiver.
A deep breath.
3 2 1
Splash!

15ᵗʰ August

I LOVE THE LIDO CAFÉ BECAUSE...
Arthur (with help from Henry) Loten

Even when it's crowded
My brother stops serving to give me hot chocolate and a hug.
I love when Max comes in too

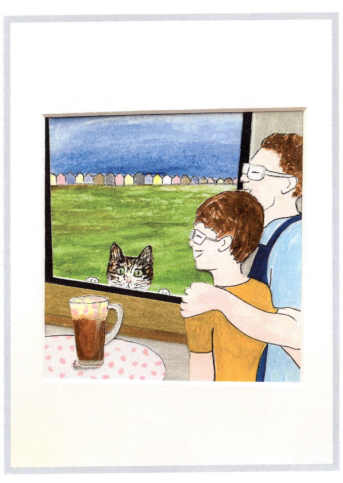

22nd August

SCHOOL DAY SWIMS

Tracy Brown

Bombing, diving, underwater hand-stands. The slide, the dive
boards and the chase with the boys.
The alternate Wednesday clean, seaweed scrubbed from the
wooden sides. The joy of 'almost' being able to see the
bottom. For a short while.
School swimming lessons with Mrs Vincent and Mr Bishop,
standing wrapped in their coats on the edge while us kids were
oblivious. To the cold water.
Sponsored swims, the significance of 72 widths. One mile.
And then there was Mavis, and aide Mrs Stocks.
Mavis. The original face of Brightlingsea Lido.

29ᵗʰ August

SWIMATHON

R.E. LOTEN

Up and down,
Arms and legs pumping furiously.
Raising both heart-rates and money,
It's Swimathon success!

5ᵗʰ September

PUTTING THE LIDO TO BED

R.E. LOTEN

Silence settles on the water
No laughing
No shouting
No splashing
A calm peace descends
And the Lido sleeps.

12th September

BRIGHTLINGSEA LIDO

PEYTON FILMER

Bright skies way up high
Reduced reasons to cry
In the cold pool we go
Going down real low
Hot fresh chips from the shop
Tomato sauce plopped on top
Lemonade very cold on ice
Ice cream so very nice
Nannas eyes are always spying
Gulls up cheekily prying
Sea and warm sand in sight
Everyone splashing with might
All faces are smiling

Lines to get in are fast piling
I don't ever want to leave
Dad thinks I'm naïve, but
Oh, how I love to be at the lido.

19ᵗʰ September

TO A LOCAL LANDMARK

D.H.L. HEWA

Light flickers and shimmers
It's a clear, calm day
Diamond shapes dance
On the water, rippling it

Bright, greeting a welcome to the
Revellers around
Ice lollies
Galore
Happiness in
The community cafe
Lifeguard in red and yellow, keeping a watchful eye, on the main pool swimmers and children paddling around, the weather and water
Inviting people in, as they flock to a local landmark, which is
Ninety years young
Going from strength to strength, now
Summer's here, at long long last
Enjoy, enjoy, enjoy
Any which way you can

26th September

MOBILITY

Linda Taglialavore

I mean, I'm not desperate. And it's only a coffee. Millions of people have coffee together, there's nothing in it, nothing at all. Just a simple cup of coffee between two people and as I am definitely NOT looking for a boyfriend, I shall keep it friendly but formal. These little tables at the LIDO café are perfect for such a rendezvous, don't want candles and pot plants giving the wrong impression. He's here, I can see the mobility scooter sweeping a bend at speed. How do I look?

3ʳᵈ October

A TYPICAL FRIDAY
IN THE CAFÉ

R.E. LOTEN

Author writing
Businessman typing
Friends chatting
Dogs munching sausages.
A community united by a café.

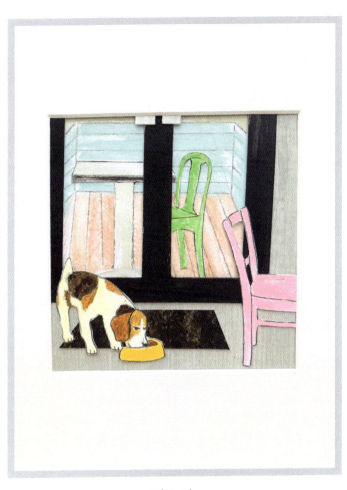

10ʰ October

I COULD WRITE
A BOOK

D.H.L. Hewa

Having survived a World War, and avoided enforced early retirement, I've reached the grand age of ninety. Days like today, crisp, clear, electric blue sky, a warming sun glistening on the water, visitors chat and laughter filling the air, their everyday routine and grind left behind, makes those times when rain, snow and wind lash down, when I'm alone, bereft of company, so worthwhile. Now listening to local gossip, sibling rivalries, family arguments, teasing banter, telling of jokes, seeing them splashing around, I could write a book of it all.

17th October

HALLOWEEN DISCO

R.E. LOTEN

The nights are getting cooler with darkness drawing in
Orange leaves are falling, time for autumn to begin
Spooky season is upon us, ghosts and ghouls abound
It's Halloween at the YMCA with a spooky disco sound.

So come on down and join us; dance to a funky beat
The Lido isn't open, but still provides a treat
There's music to dance to, drinks, snacks and fun to be had
We don't mind what you're wearing (but please ensure that
it's bad)

At the YMCA
28/10 - Save the Day!

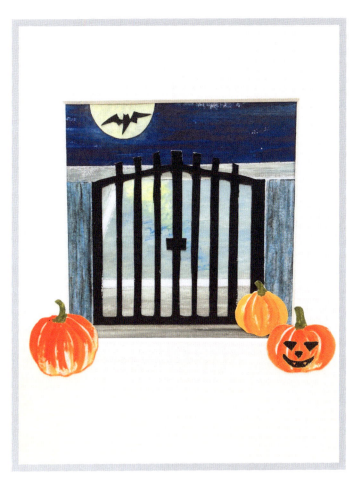

24th October

IT'S DOING ME GOOD (OR 'THE RELUCTANT SWIMMER')

James Loten

Blimey it's cold!
Right as you jump
In, but in fact it's most refreshing.
Go straight in and swim to the deep end -
Holding your breath helps
To keep you acclimatised.
Lengths. I count them down as a way to keep going -
I try to do at least ten,
Not always swimming straight or well.
Got to have a bacon sandwich afterwards,
Seems only right and proper.
Exiting the water, I feel positive,
Aware that I've swum some calories away. The

Lido
Is
Doing me good.
Of course!

31ˢᵗ October

BRIGHTLINGSEA REMEMBERS

R.E. LOTEN

At the going down of the sun
Shadows of dying light on water
Did they build it? Swim here?
We will remember them

7ᵗʰ November

AFTERNOON TEA

R.E. LOTEN

The Café lights are bright
Max is prowling.
Afternoon tea is being served.
Cake. Scones. Jam. Cream. Relax.

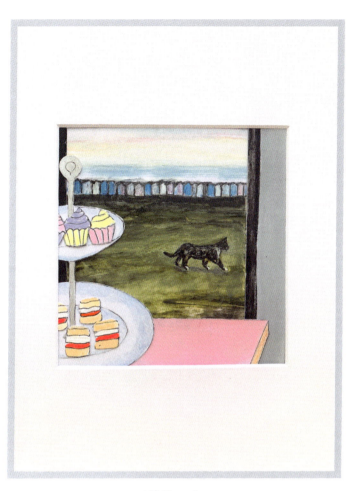

14ᵗʰ November

THAT'S NOT WHAT I MEANT!

MARK HARRISON

Meet you at the Lido, she said.
The Café?, I said.
Yes, it's a date.
A date? Not had a date for a while! I thought.

21ˢᵗ November

THE BIRDS

R.E. LOTEN

In winter as the water's low
Birds take over the Lido
Pose for photos, happy to roam
Round their borrowed home

28th November

MANY HANDS MAKE LIDO WORK

Rachel Fletcher

Many hands make Lido work
Our motto through the years*
Now we celebrate our 90th
Because of all our volunteers**

*since 2018 when we became a Charitable Incorporated
Organisation

**Including trustees and peers from other lidos, near and far,
who have supported us.

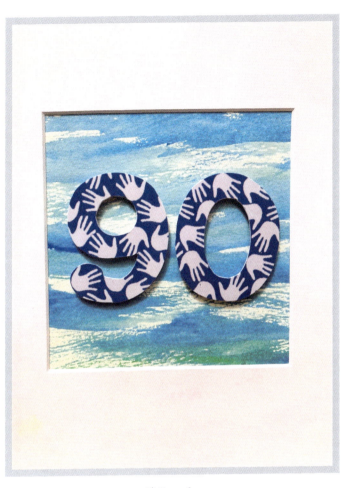

5ᵗʰ December

SEEK ME OUT

AMANDA DOLAN-HARRISON

The past. The present. The future. I've seen many trends and fashions, changing like the Essex weather, yet I endure. I'm just me, not a fancy palace like Buckingham or a national monument like the Cenotaph, or even a world heritage site like Stonehenge, but a unique, very local, jewel in my wonderful Brightlingsea community shining ever brighter as I'm continually discovered by new generations and re-visited by old friends. I'm the Lido, loud and proud, always here, yearning for your company. Be part of my history. Seek me out!

12th December

BRIGHTLINGSEA LIDO

JENNY AND MICK BARRY

Beautiful, calm, clear blue water
Red short saviours on the chair
In we go, smile and wonder!
Grab a chair, gasp and giggle
Heatwave helps
Two hundred plus, sweat and sizzle
Lifeguards watching, waiting, rotating
In at the deep end, jump and dive
No bombing, no running, on the safe side
Grinning, gurgling, splashing, splurging
Swim, sun, shade and smiles
Early swim, lane swim, moon swim, slow swim?
Accessible to all

Leaping, lying, last one in ...
Ice cream and chips
Deck chairs to lounge in
Oh what a day!

19th December

REFLECTIONS

R.E. LOTEN

A year of celebrations and success
I'm sure you'll all agree
As we say, 'Goodbye' to 2022
And, 'Hello' to 2023

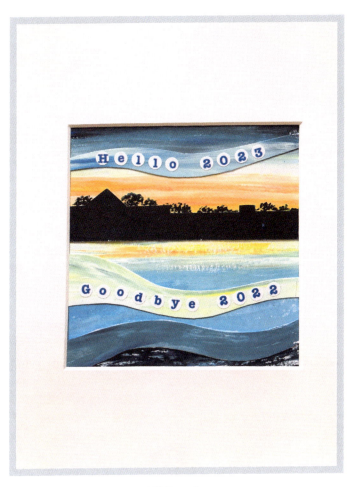

26ᵗʰ December

COMING UP
FOR AIR
Sue Davnall

Nothing had changed in forty years. Sounds of splashing and whoops of childish pleasure filtered into the cramped cubicle from beyond the swing door. Fingers of sunlight reached along the concrete floor. It was thirty degrees outside yet Jen bristled with goosebumps at the unwelcome memories.

She tugged at the crotch of her swimming costume. It was difficult these days to find something that was long enough in the body to stop it riding up at the back. She knew she shouldn't care; who'd be looking anyway? That's what Andrew always said when she was worrying about what to wear. Empathy of a rhino, that man.

'Come on, Mum. The kids are desperate to get in.'

'Alright, dear, just a sec.'

Shoving her jeans and tee-shirt into her rucksack, Jen wrapped her towel – the largest that Sainsbury's sold – under her armpits, tucking in the ends firmly. Then she performed the complicated manoeuvre of swinging her bag on her shoulder while picking up her shoes in one hand and tugging at the door with the other. There really wasn't enough room in here for such acrobatics but eventually she edged her way out.

'Good grief, Mum, what were you doing in there?'

'Sorry, love.'

Kathy strode off along the edge of the pool, young Robbie wailing as the pushchair bumped and twisted over the anti-slip surface. The twins had already scampered as far as the grass at the far end. Why couldn't her daughter keep them under control? Jen scuttled along behind Kathy as closely as she could, trying not to be noticed.

'Here, mum, this'll do.'

Kathy braked the pushchair, passing Jen a tartan rug from the tray underneath. The scorched brown grass, worn thin this late in the summer, was scratchy underfoot. Jen hitched up her towel before reaching cautiously for the rug, keeping her elbows tucked in tightly to anchor her flimsy Maginot Line of protection.

'Not there, mum, that's too close to the water.'

Jen shook out the rug, smoothing it flat over the lumpy ground. Robbie was whisked out of the pushchair and plumped, still grizzling, in the middle of the rug; Jen dropped thankfully beside him.

'Alice, Emily – come here!'

The girls ran over, already peeling off their tee-shirts. For the hundredth time, Jen marvelled that the twins looked so dissimilar. Alice was round and blonde like her mother, Emily as slight and dark as her father; she reminded Jen of a young Winona Ryder.

'Come here, sweetie, let me help you with your shorts.'

This to Alice: always the more biddable child. Emily had been distracted by the opportunity to torment her little brother.

'Gramma, will you come in the water with us?'

Jen folded Alice's discarded clothes and put them in the corner of the rug.

'I don't think so, my love. I'm not very good in the water. Mummy's a much better swimmer, she'll go with you.'

'You always say that.'

Jen saw for a moment in Alice's crestfallen face the image of Kathy at the same age. It was true what they say, the apple doesn't fall far from the tree.

'Keep an eye on Robbie for me, Mum. I'll take the kids in for a quick dip then we'll think about lunch.'

'OK, love.'

Jen stretched out on the rug, one knee raised, resting her left hand on Robbie's leg and holding the other over her eyes to keep out the glare. She'd forgotten her glasses again. Kathy had smothered the baby in sun cream: the smell of lotion, the sounds of splashing water and the warm caressing air reminded Jen of childhood holidays at the seaside with her parents and brother. An oasis of safety, away from the mockery of her schoolmates on their summer trips to the lido.

'Hey, it's Duck-face!'

'Duck feet, more like. Look at her waddle!'

'Quack quack quack!'

'Did your Mum make your swimming costume from old curtains, Duck-face?'

'Your bum's hanging out, Duck-face. Give us a wiggle.'

'The only duck that can't swim. Perhaps we should give her a swimming lesson.'

'Hey mum, you haven't fallen asleep, have you? You're looking very pink.'

Jen struggled to a sitting position. She must have dozed off without putting on any lotion – her arms and chest were the shade of one of those pink fondant fancies. Where was Robbie? Her heart began to race before she realised that he was still curled up next to her.

'Where are the girls?'

'They've gone ahead to the café.'

'On their own?'

Visions of sinister figures clutching sweets to lure away innocent kiddies rose up before Jen.

'Of course not! Bloody hell, Mum, they're only seven! What do you take me for? We ran into Debbie and her kids. The twins have gone with them. Mags is there too, Debbie's mum, remember? You coming?'

Mags. Maggie. Most glamorous girl in the class. Most persistent of Jen's tormentors. Jen had spotted her at the local cinema a few years ago – stick-thin, artfully highlighted blonde hair, immaculate make-up, same old (young) Mags. Jen had ducked around a corner in order not to be seen.

'I don't think so, Kathy, not just yet. I'll catch up with you.'

'Are you sure? You probably should get out of the sun for a bit.'

'I won't be long.'

'Suit yourself.'

Kathy swung the changing bag over her shoulder and scooped up Robbie. Jen admired her daughter's confident stride as she set off towards the café. Kathy was pretty solidly built – her mother's daughter – but had never seemed in the slightest bit concerned by it. Jen envied her.

Jen lay down again and daydreamed about her forth-coming wedding anniversary. Thirty years! What was the chance of Andrew actually pulling his finger out and planning something special? Zilch, really. It would have been lovely just for once to have left everything to him but it wasn't going to happen ...

Jen realised that she'd been feeling increasingly uncomfort-able for the past few minutes. One of the curses of middle age was that the urge to go arrived suddenly and with great urgency. Now where were the loos? Next to the changing rooms, she'd need to walk back round.

She scrambled to her feet and enveloped herself in her towel. Her eyes darting around to check for onlookers, she stepped towards the path around the edge of the pool, glancing sideways into the water as she did so. There was a dark shape on the bottom, a deflated float or li-lo. Fronds swirled slowly in the water.

Then Jen heard a shout from the far end; looking up she saw a lifeguard on the point of leaping into action, surrounded by a small group of women gesticulating frantically and pointing to just below where Jen was standing. Peering down again, her perspective shifted: now she saw that the 'float' was a small child, motionless on the bottom of the pool. The lifeguard had grabbed a long pole with a hoop on the end and was running full tilt towards her. But he looked so far away.

Without calculation, Jen tore off her towel and jumped in. The pool was heated yet the coldness of the water in contrast with the hot sun stopped Jen's breath in her throat. She had no idea how to upend herself and dive to the bottom so she just let herself sink, flapping her hands to speed up her descent. She groped around with her feet until she felt something then reached down. Pulling slowly – she had hold of the child's hair - she drew the small body into her arms. At the same moment, she felt herself grasped by the waist and propelled upwards. As she reached the surface others lifted the child from her arms onto the side of the pool. The lifeguard jack-knifed out of the water.

'Stand back! Back! Someone call for an ambulance!'

Jen reached for the side of the pool. She was disorientated, the bile was rising in her stomach. Now that the moment was passed she shuddered with cold and fear.

'And help the woman! Get her out of there.'

Jen was conscious enough to experience in full the humiliation of being hauled out of the water like a giant fish until she was lying on the hard concrete gasping for air.

'Anyone got a towel?'

'Sit her up.'

'Get her a hot drink.'

'Mum? Mum!'

Kathy was kneeling beside her, hugging her until she felt her ribs would break. Jen couldn't remember the last time that Kathy had embraced her like she meant it. The nee-naw of an approaching ambulance prompted Jen to look over at the prone form.

'How is he? She?'

The lifeguard looked up. Jen could see now that the child was a small girl, her dark hair spread around her like seaweed. She was beginning to move her limbs: stuttering sobs led into a full-throated wail of 'Mummy!!!!'.

'She's doing very well, madam. She wasn't in there long enough to do much damage. We're just getting her to hospital as a precaution.'

Jen suddenly felt very tired.

The ambulance had been and gone and Jen had been taken to the café. Still wrapped in someone else's towel, she sipped at a too-hot hot chocolate that the manageress had pushed into her hands. A plate of sweet biscuits sat at her elbow. Raheem, the lifeguard, patted her shoulder as he sat down beside her.

'That was a very brave thing that you did, Mrs Brown. But very foolhardy too. We might have been sending two of you to hospital, you know.'

'I didn't think. It could have been one of my grandkids. It just... happened.'

'I understand that. But it's never a good idea to jump in like that. Far better to try to reach them from dry land if they've fallen in. People don't think about the impact the change in temperature can have – it could knock you out cold if you're unlucky. And if it was a river or the sea there's currents, things underwater to catch your foot in, all sorts. If I were you – '

'I'm sorry, Raheem, could I just have a word with Mrs Brown a minute?'

The manageress was standing with mobile phone in hand, smiling expectantly.

'Yeah, sure.'

'Would you mind if we took a couple of pictures, Mrs Brown? For the local press? You're quite the celebrity you know.'

She gestured at the crowd of onlookers at the other end of the café.

'I don't know, I don't think so, I'm a bit of a mess.'

'I could give you a few minutes to straighten yourself up a bit if you want to. But it really doesn't matter. You're the woman of the moment, no-one cares if you're a bit dishevelled, it's what you did that counts.'

Jen hesitated, then looked round at her fan club. There in the front row was Mags, gazing at her with undiluted admiration.

'OK then.'

Printed in Great Britain
by Amazon

32085425R00075